Circus Training Journal

Three Month Journal
(five weeks per month)

Created by Rebecca Starr & Thom Wall,
with developmental support by Sarah Baker

Modern Vaudeville Press

Month at a Glance

M	T	W

This month's big goal:

Month:

Th	F	S / Su

This month's mantra:

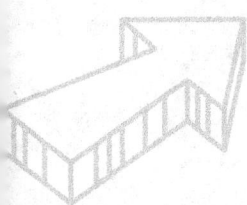

Monthly Habit Tracker

1										
2										
3										
4										
5										
6										
7										
8										
9										
10										
11										
12										
13										
14										
15										

Daily habits:

-
-
-
-
-
-
-
-
-

Month:

16									
17									
18									
19									
20									
21									
22									
23									
24									
25									
26									
27									
28									
29									
30									
31									

This month's smaller goals:
-
-
-
-
-
-
-
-
-

Weekly Activities

Mon

Tues

Wed

Thurs

Fri

Sat

Sun

Week of:

Weekly goals

Weekly to-dos

This week, I want to do... I want to feel...

Energy Intake & Hydration

Day	Food	H$_2$O	Time
Mon			
Breakfast			
Snack			
Lunch			
Snack			
Dinner			
Tues			
Wed			

Week of:

Day	Food	H$_2$O	Time
Thurs			
Fri			
Sat			
Sun			

Sleep Log

	Mon	Tues	Wed
Wake time			
Resting HR			
Hours slept			
Soreness level			
Fatigue level			
Sleep quality			
Notes			
Sleep time			

Week of:

Thurs	Fri	Sat	Sun

Conditioning Workouts

Notes	Exercise

Week of:

Sets	Reps	M	T	W	Th	F	S	Su

Specialty Workouts

Notes	Exercise

Week of:

Sets	Reps	M	T	W	Th	F	S	Su

Specialty Workouts

Notes	Exercise

Week of:

Sets	Reps	M	T	W	Th	F	S	Su

Specialty Workouts

Notes	Exercise

Week of:

Sets	Reps	M	T	W	Th	F	S	Su

End of Week Reflections

What worked this week?

What didn't work this week?

Did I honor the process?

Week of:

Observations

Breakthroughs

Notes

Week of:

Notes

Week of:

Week of:

Weekly Activities

Mon	Thurs

Tues	Fri

Wed	Sat
	Sun

Week of:

Weekly goals

Weekly to-dos

This week, I want to do... I want to feel...

Energy Intake & Hydration

Day	Food	H₂O	Time
Mon			
Breakfast			
Snack			
Lunch			
Snack			
Dinner			
Tues			
Wed			

Week of:

Day	Food	H$_2$O	Time
Thurs			
Fri			
Sat			
Sun			

Sleep Log

	Mon	Tues	Wed
Wake time			
Resting HR			
Hours slept			
Soreness level			
Fatigue level			
Sleep quality			
Notes			
Sleep time			

Week of:

Thurs	Fri	Sat	Sun

Conditioning Workouts

Notes	Exercise

Week of:

Sets	Reps	M	T	W	Th	F	S	Su

Specialty Workouts

Notes	Exercise

Week of:

Sets	Reps	M	T	W	Th	F	S	Su

Specialty Workouts

Notes	Exercise

Week of:

Sets	Reps	M	T	W	Th	F	S	Su

Specialty Workouts

Notes	Exercise

Week of:

Sets	Reps	M	T	W	Th	F	S	Su

End of Week Reflections

What worked this week?

What didn't work this week?

Did I honor the process?

Week of:

Observations

Breakthroughs

Notes

Notes

Week of:

Week of:

Weekly Activities

Mon	Thurs

Tues	Fri

Wed	Sat
	Sun

Week of:

Weekly goals

Weekly to-dos

This week, I want to do... I want to feel...

Energy Intake & Hydration

Day	Food	H$_2$O	Time
Mon			
Breakfast			
Snack			
Lunch			
Snack			
Dinner			
Tues			
Wed			

Week of:

Day	Food	H₂O	Time
Thurs			
Fri			
Sat			
Sun			

Sleep Log

	Mon	Tues	Wed
Wake time			
Resting HR			
Hours slept			
Soreness level			
Fatigue level			
Sleep quality			
Notes			
Sleep time			

Week of:

Thurs	Fri	Sat	Sun

Conditioning Workouts

Notes	Exercise

Week of:

Sets	Reps	M	T	W	Th	F	S	Su

Specialty Workouts

Notes	Exercise

Week of:

Sets	Reps	M	T	W	Th	F	S	Su

Specialty Workouts

Notes | Exercise

Week of:

Sets	Reps	M	T	W	Th	F	S	Su

Specialty Workouts

Notes | Exercise

Week of:

Sets	Reps	M	T	W	Th	F	S	Su

End of Week Reflections

What worked this week?

What didn't work this week?

Did I honor the process?

Week of:

Observations

Breakthroughs

Notes

Week of:

Notes

Week of:

Week of:

Weekly Activities

Mon	Thurs

Tues	Fri

Wed	Sat
	Sun

Week of:

Weekly goals

Weekly to-dos

This week, I want to do... I want to feel...

Energy Intake & Hydration

Day	Food	H$_2$O	Time
Mon			
Breakfast			
Snack			
Lunch			
Snack			
Dinner			
Tues			
Wed			

Week of:

Day	Food	H₂O	Time
Thurs			
Fri			
Sat			
Sun			

Sleep Log

	Mon	Tues	Wed
Wake time			
Resting HR			
Hours slept			
Soreness level			
Fatigue level			
Sleep quality			
Notes			
Sleep time			

Week of:

Thurs	Fri	Sat	Sun

Conditioning Workouts

Notes	Exercise

Week of:

Sets	Reps	M	T	W	Th	F	S	Su

Specialty Workouts

Notes	Exercise

Week of:

Sets	Reps	M	T	W	Th	F	S	Su

Specialty Workouts

Notes	Exercise

Week of:

Sets	Reps	M	T	W	Th	F	S	Su

Specialty Workouts

Notes	Exercise

Week of:

Sets	Reps	M	T	W	Th	F	S	Su

End of Week Reflections

What worked this week?

What didn't work this week?

Did I honor the process?

Week of:

Observations

Breakthroughs

Notes

Week of:

Week of:

Notes

Weekly Activities

Mon	Thurs

Tues	Fri

Wed	Sat
	Sun

Week of:

Weekly goals

Weekly to-dos

This week, I want to do... I want to feel...

Energy Intake & Hydration

Day	Food	H₂O	Time
Mon			
Breakfast			
Snack			
Lunch			
Snack			
Dinner			
Tues			
Wed			

Week of:

Day	Food	H$_2$O	Time
Thurs			
Fri			
Sat			
Sun			

Sleep Log

	Mon	Tues	Wed
Wake time			
Resting HR			
Hours slept			
Soreness level			
Fatigue level			
Sleep quality			
Notes			
Sleep time			

Week of:

Thurs	Fri	Sat	Sun

Conditioning Workouts

Notes	Exercise

Week of:

Sets	Reps	M	T	W	Th	F	S	Su

Specialty Workouts

Notes	Exercise

Week of:

Sets	Reps	M	T	W	Th	F	S	Su

Specialty Workouts

Notes	Exercise

Week of:

Sets	Reps	M	T	W	Th	F	S	Su

Specialty Workouts

Notes	Exercise

Week of:

Sets	Reps	M	T	W	Th	F	S	Su

End of Week Reflections

What worked this week?

What didn't work this week?

Did I honor the process?

Week of:

Observations

Breakthroughs

Notes

Week of:

Week of:

Week of:

Did I notice progress in my [...]

Am I making the best use of my training time?

Am I owning myself credit for how well I am doing?

How can I improve next month?

End of Month Reflections

Did I notice progress in my training this month?

Am I making the best use of my training time?

Am I giving myself credit for the work I am doing?

How can I improve next month?

Week of:

Week of:

Month at a Glance

M	T	W

This month's big goal:

Month:

Th	F	S / Su

This month's mantra:

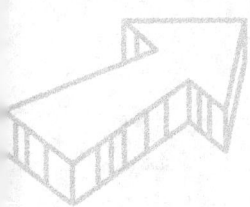

Monthly Habit Tracker

1										
2										
3										
4										
5										
6										
7										
8										
9										
10										
11										
12										
13										
14										
15										

Daily habits:

-
-
-
-
-
-
-
-
-

Month:

16									
17									
18									
19									
20									
21									
22									
23									
24									
25									
26									
27									
28									
29									
30									
31									

This month's smaller goals:
-
-
-
-
-
-
-
-
-

Weekly Activities

Mon

Tues

Wed

Thurs

Fri

Sat

Sun

Week of:

Weekly goals

Weekly to-dos

This week, I want to do... I want to feel...

Energy Intake & Hydration

Day	Food	H₂O	Time
Mon			
Breakfast			
Snack			
Lunch			
Snack			
Dinner			
Tues			
Wed			

Week of:

Day	Food	H₂O	Time
Thurs			
Fri			
Sat			
Sun			

Sleep Log

	Mon	Tues	Wed
Wake time			
Resting HR			
Hours slept			
Soreness level			
Fatigue level			
Sleep quality			
Notes			
Sleep time			

Week of:

Thurs	Fri	Sat	Sun

Conditioning Workouts

Notes	Exercise

Specialty Workout

Week of:

Sets	Reps	M	T	W	Th	F	S	Su

Specialty Workouts

Notes	Exercise

Week of:

Sets	Reps	M	T	W	Th	F	S	Su

Specialty Workouts

Notes		Exercise

Week of:

Sets	Reps	M	T	W	Th	F	S	Su

Specialty Workouts

Notes	Exercise

Week of:

Sets	Reps	M	T	W	Th	F	S	Su

End of Week Reflections

What worked this week?

What didn't work this week?

Did I honor the process?

Week of:

Observations

Breakthroughs

Notes

Notes

Notes

Weekly Activities

Mon	Thurs

Tues	Fri

Wed	Sat
	Sun

Week of:

Weekly goals

Weekly to-dos

This week, I want to do... I want to feel...

Energy Intake & Hydration

Day	Food	H$_2$O	Time
Mon			
Breakfast			
Snack			
Lunch			
Snack			
Dinner			
Tues			
Wed			

Week of:

Day	Food	H₂O	Time
Thurs			
Fri			
Sat			
Sun			

Sleep Log

	Mon	Tues	Wed
Wake time			
Resting HR			
Hours slept			
Soreness level			
Fatigue level			
Sleep quality			
Notes			
Sleep time			

Week of:

Thurs	Fri	Sat	Sun

Conditioning Workouts

Notes	Exercise

Week of:

Sets	Reps	M	T	W	Th	F	S	Su	

Specialty Workouts

Notes	Exercise

Week of:

Sets	Reps	M	T	W	Th	F	S	Su

Specialty Workouts

Notes	Exercise

Week of:

Sets	Reps	M	T	W	Th	F	S	Su

Specialty Workouts

Notes	Exercise

Week of:

Sets	Reps	M	T	W	Th	F	S	Su	

End of Week Reflections

What worked this week?

What didn't work this week?

Did I honor the process?

Week of:

Observations

Breakthroughs

Week of:

Notes

Week of:

Weekly Activities

Mon	Thurs

Tues	Fri

Wed	Sat
	Sun

Week of:

Weekly goals

Weekly to-dos

This week, I want to do... I want to feel...

Energy Intake & Hydration

Day	Food	H$_2$O	Time
Mon			
Breakfast			
Snack			
Lunch			
Snack			
Dinner			
Tues			
Wed			

Week of:

Day	Food	H$_2$O	Time
Thurs			
Fri			
Sat			
Sun			

Sleep Log

	Mon	Tues	Wed
Wake time			
Resting HR			
Hours slept			
Soreness level			
Fatigue level			
Sleep quality			
Notes			
Sleep time			

Week of:

Thurs	Fri	Sat	Sun

Conditioning Workouts

Notes	Exercise

Week of:

Sets	Reps	M	T	W	Th	F	S	Su

Specialty Workouts

Notes	Exercise

Week of:

Sets	Reps	M	T	W	Th	F	S	Su

Specialty Workouts

Notes	Exercise

Specialty Workout

Week of:

Sets	Reps	M	T	W	Th	F	S	Su

Specialty Workouts

Notes	Exercise

Week of:

Sets	Reps	M	T	W	Th	F	S	Su	

End of Week Reflections

What worked this week?

What didn't work this week?

Did I honor the process?

Week of:

Observations

Breakthroughs

Notes

Week of:

Week of:

Weekly Activities

Mon

Tues

Wed

Thurs

Fri

Sat

Sun

Week of:

Weekly goals

Weekly to-dos

This week, I want to do... I want to feel...

Energy Intake & Hydration

Day	Food	H$_2$O	Time
Mon			
Breakfast			
Snack			
Lunch			
Snack			
Dinner			
Tues			
Wed			

Week of:

Day	Food	H₂O	Time
Thurs			
Fri			
Sat			
Sun			

Sleep Log

	Mon	Tues	Wed
Wake time			
Resting HR			
Hours slept			
Soreness level			
Fatigue level			
Sleep quality			
Notes			
Sleep time			

Week of:

Thurs	Fri	Sat	Sun

Conditioning Workouts

Notes	Exercise

Week of:

Sets	Reps	M	T	W	Th	F	S	Su

Specialty Workouts

Notes	Exercise

Week of:

Sets	Reps	M	T	W	Th	F	S	Su

Specialty Workouts

Notes	Exercise

Week of:

Sets	Reps	M	T	W	Th	F	S	Su

Specialty Workouts

Notes	Exercise

Week of:

Sets	Reps	M	T	W	Th	F	S	Su

End of Week Reflections

What worked this week?

What didn't work this week?

Did I honor the process?

Week of:

Observations

Breakthroughs

Week of:

Week of:

Notes

Weekly Activities

Mon	Thurs

Tues	Fri

Wed	Sat
	Sun

Week of:

Weekly goals

Weekly to-dos

This week, I want to do... I want to feel...

Energy Intake & Hydration

Day	Food	H$_2$O	Time
Mon			
Breakfast			
Snack			
Lunch			
Snack			
Dinner			
Tues			
Wed			

Week of:

Day	Food	H$_2$O	Time
Thurs			
Fri			
Sat			
Sun			

Sleep Log

	Mon	Tues	Wed
Wake time			
Resting HR			
Hours slept			
Soreness level			
Fatigue level			
Sleep quality			
Notes			
Sleep time			

Week of:

Thurs	Fri	Sat	Sun

Conditioning Workouts

Notes | Exercise

Week of:

Sets	Reps	M	T	W	Th	F	S	Su

Specialty Workouts

Notes	Exercise

Week of:

Sets	Reps	M	T	W	Th	F	S	Su

Specialty Workouts

Notes	Exercise

Week of:

	Sets	Reps	M	T	W	Th	F	S	Su

Specialty Workouts

Notes	Exercise

Week of:

Sets	Reps	M	T	W	Th	F	S	Su

End of Week Reflections

What worked this week?

What didn't work this week?

Did I honor the process?

Week of:

Observations

Breakthroughs

Week of:

Notes

Week of:

End of Month Reflections

Week of:

What notable progress is in my routine this mo.?

Am I making the best use of my cooking time?

Am I giving myself credit for the work I am doing?

How can I improve next month?

End of Month Reflections

Did I notice progress in my training this month?

Am I making the best use of my training time?

Am I giving myself credit for the work I am doing?

How can I improve next month?

Week of:

Notes

Week of:

Month at a Glance

M	T	W

This month's big goal:

Month:

Th	F	S / Su

This month's mantra:

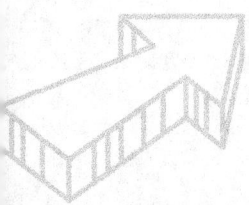

Monthly Habit Tracker

1										
2										
3										
4										
5										
6										
7										
8										
9										
10										
11										
12										
13										
14										
15										

Daily habits:

-
-
-
-
-
-
-
-
-

Month:

16									
17									
18									
19									
20									
21									
22									
23									
24									
25									
26									
27									
28									
29									
30									
31									

This month's smaller goals:
-
-
-
-
-
-
-
-
-

Weekly Activities

Mon	Thurs

Tues	Fri

Wed	Sat
	Sun

Week of:

Weekly goals

Weekly to-dos

This week, I want to do... I want to feel...

Energy Intake & Hydration

Day	Food	H₂O	Time
Mon			
Breakfast			
Snack			
Lunch			
Snack			
Dinner			
Tues			
Wed			

Week of:

Day	Food	H₂O	Time
Thurs			
Fri			
Sat			
Sun			

Sleep Log

	Mon	Tues	Wed
Wake time			
Resting HR			
Hours slept			
Soreness level			
Fatigue level			
Sleep quality			
Notes			
Sleep time			

Week of:

Thurs	Fri	Sat	Sun

Conditioning Workouts

Notes | Exercise

Specialty Workout

Week of:

Sets	Reps	M	T	W	Th	F	S	Su

Specialty Workouts

Notes | Exercise

Week of:

Sets	Reps	M	T	W	Th	F	S	Su

Specialty Workouts

Notes	Exercise

Week of:

Sets	Reps	M	T	W	Th	F	S	Su

Specialty Workouts

Notes	Exercise

Week of:

Sets	Reps	M	T	W	Th	F	S	Su	

End of Week Reflections

What worked this week?

What didn't work this week?

Did I honor the process?

Week of:

Observations

Breakthroughs

Week of:

Week of:

Week of:

Weekly Activities

Mon	Thurs

Tues	Fri

Wed	Sat
	Sun

Week of:

Weekly goals

Weekly to-dos

This week, I want to do... I want to feel...

Energy Intake & Hydration

Day	Food	H₂O	Time
Mon			
Breakfast			
Snack			
Lunch			
Snack			
Dinner			
Tues			
Wed			

Week of:

Day	Food	H₂O	Time
Thurs			
Fri			
Sat			
Sun			

Sleep Log

	Mon	Tues	Wed
Wake time			
Resting HR			
Hours slept			
Soreness level			
Fatigue level			
Sleep quality			
Notes			
Sleep time			

Week of:

Thurs	Fri	Sat	Sun

Conditioning Workouts

Notes	Exercise

Week of:

Sets	Reps	M	T	W	Th	F	S	Su

Specialty Workouts

Notes	Exercise

Week of:

Sets	Reps	M	T	W	Th	F	S	Su

Specialty Workouts

Notes | Exercise

Week of:

Sets	Reps	M	T	W	Th	F	S	Su

Specialty Workouts

Notes	Exercise

Week of:

Sets	Reps	M	T	W	Th	F	S	Su

End of Week Reflections

What worked this week?

What didn't work this week?

Did I honor the process?

Week of:

Observations

Breakthroughs

Notes

Week of:

Week of:

Week of:

Weekly Activities

Mon	Thurs

Tues	Fri

Wed	Sat
	Sun

Week of:

Weekly goals

Weekly to-dos

This week, I want to do... I want to feel...

Energy Intake & Hydration

Day	Food	H$_2$O	Time
Mon			
Breakfast			
Snack			
Lunch			
Snack			
Dinner			
Tues			
Wed			

Week of:

Day	Food	H₂O	Time
Thurs			
Fri			
Sat			
Sun			

Sleep Log

	Mon	Tues	Wed
Wake time			
Resting HR			
Hours slept			
Soreness level			
Fatigue level			
Sleep quality			
Notes			
Sleep time			

Week of:

Thurs	Fri	Sat	Sun

Conditioning Workouts

Notes | Exercise

Week of:

Sets	Reps	M	T	W	Th	F	S	Su

Specialty Workouts

Notes	Exercise

Week of:

Sets	Reps	M	T	W	Th	F	S	Su

Specialty Workouts

Notes	Exercise

Speciality Workout

Week of:

Sets	Reps	M	T	W	Th	F	S	Su

Specialty Workouts

Notes	Exercise

Week of:

Sets	Reps	M	T	W	Th	F	S	Su

End of Week Reflections

What worked this week?

What didn't work this week?

Did I honor the process?

Week of:

Observations

Breakthroughs

Week of:

Week of:

Weekly Activities

Mon

Tues

Wed

Thurs

Fri

Sat

Sun

Week of:

Weekly goals

Weekly to-dos

This week, I want to do... I want to feel...

Energy Intake & Hydration

Day	Food	H₂O	Time
Mon			
Breakfast			
Snack			
Lunch			
Snack			
Dinner			
Tues			
Wed			

Week of:

Day	Food	H$_2$O	Time
Thurs			
Fri			
Sat			
Sun			

Sleep Log

	Mon	Tues	Wed
Wake time			
Resting HR			
Hours slept			
Soreness level			
Fatigue level			
Sleep quality			
Notes			
Sleep time			

Week of:

Thurs	Fri	Sat	Sun

Conditioning Workouts

Notes	Exercise

Week of:

Sets	Reps	M	T	W	Th	F	S	Su

Specialty Workouts

Notes	Exercise

Week of:

Sets	Reps	M	T	W	Th	F	S	Su

Specialty Workouts

Notes	Exercise

Week of:

Sets	Reps	M	T	W	Th	F	S	Su

Specialty Workouts

Notes	Exercise

Week of:

Sets	Reps	M	T	W	Th	F	S	Su

End of Week Reflections

What worked this week?

What didn't work this week?

Did I honor the process?

Week of:

Observations

Breakthroughs

Notes

Week of:

Notes

Week of:

Weekly Activities

Mon

Tues

Wed

Thurs

Fri

Sat

Sun

Week of:

Weekly goals

Weekly to-dos

This week, I want to do... I want to feel...

Energy Intake & Hydration

Day	Food	H$_2$O	Time
Mon			
Breakfast			
Snack			
Lunch			
Snack			
Dinner			
Tues			
Wed			

Sleep Log

Week of:

Day	Food	H$_2$O	Time
Thurs			
Fri			
Sat			
Sun			

Sleep Log

	Mon	Tues	Wed
Wake time			
Resting HR			
Hours slept			
Soreness level			
Fatigue level			
Sleep quality			
Notes			
Sleep time			

Week of:

Thurs	Fri	Sat	Sun

Conditioning Workouts

Notes	Exercise

Week of:

Sets	Reps	M	T	W	Th	F	S	Su

Specialty Workouts

Notes	Exercise

Week of:

Sets	Reps	M	T	W	Th	F	S	Su

Specialty Workouts

Notes | Exercise

Week of:

Sets	Reps	M	T	W	Th	F	S	Su

Specialty Workouts

Notes	Exercise

Week of:

Sets	Reps	M	T	W	Th	F	S	Su	

End of Week Reflections

What worked this week?

What didn't work this week?

Did I honor the process?

Week of:

Observations

Breakthroughs

Notes

Week of:

Week of:

End of Month Reflections

Week of:

Did I make progress on my goals this month?

Am I making the best use of my tutoring time?

Am I giving myself credit for the work I am doing?

How can I improve next month?

End of Month Reflections

Did I notice progress in my training this month?

Am I making the best use of my training time?

Am I giving myself credit for the work I am doing?

How can I improve next month?

Notes

Week of:

Notes

www.ingramcontent.com/pod-product-compliance
Lightning Source LLC
Chambersburg PA
CBHW012208090526
44583CB00023BA/2952